The
Wish Book
2007

The
Wish Book
2007

by
Barbel Mohr
and Pierre Franckh

HAY HOUSE
Australia • Canada • Hong Kong
South Africa • United Kingdom • United States

First published and distributed in the United Kingdom by:
Hay House UK Ltd, 292B Kensal Rd, London W10 5BE.
Tel.: (44) 20 8962 1230; Fax: (44) 20 8962 1239. www.hayhouse.co.uk

Published and distributed in the United States of America by:
Hay House, Inc., PO Box 5100, Carlsbad, CA 92018-5100.
Tel.: (1) 760 431 7695 or (800) 654 5126; Fax: (1) 760 431 6948 or
(800) 650 5115. www.hayhouse.com

Published and distributed in Australia by:
Hay House Australia Ltd, 18/36 Ralph St, Alexandria NSW 2015.
Tel.: (61) 2 9669 4299; Fax: (61) 2 9669 4144. www.hayhouse.com.au

Published and distributed in the Republic of South Africa by:
Hay House SA (Pty), Ltd, PO Box 990, Witkoppen 2068.
Tel./Fax: (27) 11 706 6612. orders@psdprom.co.za

Distributed in Canada by:
Raincoast, 9050 Shaughnessy St, Vancouver, BC V6P 6E5.
Tel.: (1) 604 323 7100; Fax: (1) 604 323 2600

© Barbel Mohr and Pierre Franckh, 2006

The moral rights of the authors have been asserted.

The author of this book does not dispense medical advice or prescribe the use of any technique as a form of treatment for physical or medical problems without the advice of a physician, either directly or indirectly. The intent of the author is only to offer information of a general nature to help you in your quest for emotional and spiritual wellbeing. In the event you use any of the information in this book for yourself, which is your constitutional right, the author and the publisher assume no responsibility for your actions.

A catalogue record for this book is available from the British Library.

Cover Design: Leanne Siu
Interior Design: Leanne Siu/e-Digital Design
Illustrations: Juliet Percival

ISBN 1-4019-1531-0
ISBN 978-1-4019-1531-5

Printed and bound in Great Britain by TJ International, Padstow, Cornwall.

Contents

Barbel Mohr and her Cosmic Ordering

☆☆☆☆

Barbel Mohr used to be a photo journalist, a photographic editor and a graphic designer. She started writing in 1995, initially just as a hobby. Her first book, *The Cosmic Ordering Service (Bestellungen beim Universum)*, became an instant bestseller. So far, over a million copies have been sold, and the feedback of many of her readers shows clearly how well this method of expressing wishes works. For over ten years now she has been holding lectures and workshops. The most successful of them, and a classic by now, is a seminar on the zest for life, the *joie de vivre*, but there are others dealing with 'the hotline to heaven'.

'I discovered wishing and ordering for myself about 15 years ago. Before that I never believed in anything like that and had therefore prevented myself from having access to this wonderful world of possibilities and opportunities.

'Looking at the experiences of all my friends and my readers, it becomes clear that what is true in life in general also rings true for wishing and ordering: "Together we are stronger." Whenever we have expressed wishes together, whether individual ones or communally for one person, the success rate was in most cases even higher.'

For more information on Barbel, go to:
www.barbelmohr.de

Pierre Franckh on Successful Wishing

☆ ☆ ☆ ☆

Pierre Franckh, a writer and actor, has been interested in psychology, relationships and eroticism for a long time, resulting in bestselling books on happiness in love *(Glücksregeln für die Liebe)*, how to make love with love *(Lustvoll lieben)*, and successful wishing *(Erfolgreich wünschen)*.

Even as a child he knew instinctively how to make wishes come true. For example, he had a strong desire to play a part in a movie and promptly got one of the leading roles in a German children's classic, Ludwig Thoma's *Lausbubengeschichten*. When growing up he lost his magical knowledge somewhat and followed a more rational scepticism. Only when he later went through a life crisis did he rediscover his capacity for successful wishing. For over 30 years now it has been part and parcel of his life. In seminars and lectures Pierre Franckh keeps inspiring others with his knowledge and experience. He demonstrates convincingly that everything in life is possible if the wish for it is expressed appropriately. Scores of enthusiastic readers confirm that his simple rules for right wishing work for everyone.

Further information on: www.Pierre-Franckh.de

Wishes come true

Every day, every minute, every second.

We are constantly wishing for something,

Whether consciously or not.

We are even wishing when we don't want to wish.

What is your wish?

What do you want to bring into your life?

The How To of
Successful Wishing

☆☆☆☆

From Pierre Franckh's *Erfolgreich wünschen*.

1. Start small ...

... and convince yourself on the basis of the first good results that wishing is a reliable method. Nothing is as successful as success itself, because it nurtures further success.

2. Choose the right words

Always express a wish in the present, never in the future tense, e.g. say 'I am rich,' rather than 'I will be rich.' Otherwise we create a condition of wanting instead of being.

Pretend! We have already got what we want. We keep dealing with the things to come in a positive way and prepare ourselves in hopeful expectation. Thus we are creating the right vibrations for ourselves and practically 'draw' the event into our life.

There is no 'none' or 'don'ts' in wishing. Whatever we wish to avoid, we draw it into our lives because we invest mental energy into it. For that reason, fear attracts exactly those events we want to prevent. 'I don't want to be ill' means, as a wishful energy, 'I want to be ill.'

It's not possible to make something *not* happen. We can only create, not 'non-create'. The thought of 'non-creating' alone creates the unwanted, because our thoughts and energy are anxious. Wanting to avoid something doesn't work for that reason. But we can make the opposite happen. We simply have to focus our energy on its positive counterpart: 'I am healthy.' This order is simple and clear. Wishing that way, we are thinking of our health and not of a sickness.

Write down your wish. By writing down a wish we manifest our intention. From now on it is real. It is our firm decision. Unshakeable, clear and unequivocal.

From now on we can monitor when the wish comes true. What exactly did I wish for, and how can I change the words so that I get exactly what I have been desiring from the bottom of my heart? Also, by writing down a wish, working on it becomes much easier. This book has been especially designed for this purpose.

Express the wish clearly, precisely and briefly. The more succinctly you have expressed your wish, the more reliably your order will be carried out. If you are forced to express yourself in a short and precise way, you are forced to get to the core of your request. If you can express something in two words, you know much better in your heart what you really want.

3. Be grateful

With gratitude we increase the good things …

… because we are beginning to look at the aspects in our life that are going well. We dedicate our attention and respect to them. Whatever you focus on you dedicate energy to. By expressing gratefulness we increase all the good things that are already present in our life because we direct even more energy towards them.

Gratitude brings the wish into the present.

You could compare saying thanks with saying Amen at the end of a prayer. Amen literally translated means 'Sure, certainly!' So may it be now!

The energy in praying and wishing is very similar. In both cases we appeal to a higher force and ask for a solution. In both cases we put a seal to it and confirm it with an Amen or a thank you.

Gratitude removes all doubts and worries.

You believe in the good outcome. You are certain. In every-day life people always thank you for things that so far have not happened. 'Thank you for doing this for me!' You express gratitude for things that you are absolutely certain will be happening. The matter has been sealed. Thanking is like a signature under an important document.

4. Trust instead of doubt

A doubt is a very clear wish that will be carried out. Doubting means that we recall our wishes as soon as they have been sent. Often people say, 'It won't happen anyway!' as soon as they have thought or expressed a wish. But this thought, too, is nothing but an expressed wish. And it says: 'It won't work.' The result of it? This wish will be sent just as the other one. We are always successful – most of the time in creating our own misfortune. If you don't believe in success, you won't be successful. For that reason you have to trust fully that your wish will be granted.

5. Be discrete

Talking about your wishes weakens them. For one thing, the energy evaporates by talking about it incessantly. And we very quickly call forth all our enemies, people who are envious and doubtful, and make space for their beliefs and convictions.

6. Forget

Forgetting has more than one advantage. First, in forgetting the wish we also forget to doubt and thereby involuntarily reverse our order. Apart from that, by forgetting we prove how much we trust, because we are so certain that the wish will come true that we stop thinking about it. That way we are open to accepting the wish into our life – no matter how dismal our present situation may be.

7. Be open for coincidences

You never know in what way the wish will be delivered. Nearly always wishes are granted in a way that we never thought possible. All you have to do is be prepared for the wish to come true. The cosmos tends to find its own ways – and we cannot possibly know what these ways are.

8. Trust your intuition

As all this is a question of energies, sometimes we are guided in a very gentle way to where we will find the desired goal. You simply have to remain alert and attentive once the wish has been sent, and you will receive all the necessary information. If you manage to get in touch with your intuition, all you have to do is to follow what feels right and good.

9. Find out your truly important wishes

The main question really is: what kinds of wishes are good for me? It doesn't make sense to wish for something that has nothing to do with you and your nature – but most people tend to do just that. Often we express a wish only because other people have or enjoy the same thing. Often we chase after an ideal that has nothing to do with our lives. So, before we express and send a wish we should be clear about what we really, really need in our life. Would we really feel better, more accepted, more loved and happy? Every successful wish will change our circumstances profoundly. For that reason we should examine closely whether we are really prepared for such changes. Find out about your real, important desires and wishes so that they will actually make you happy.

How to Make the Most of this Book

☆☆☆☆

The best aspect of this *Wish Book* is that we are given the chance to learn to wish in the most perfect way.

1. First things first – write down your wish in this book

By doing this the wish will become reinforced. For the first time it will leave our body in a physical way. That alone will lend it power and strength. Suddenly we mean it seriously. We are no longer in the realm of speculation and dreams where we never really believe in anything. It is now in the material world. It is our formed intention. Unshakeable, clear and unequivocal.

If we kept on wishing throughout our lives, at some point we would forget all the things we wished for in the past and lose touch with all of them. Apart from that, we don't always and consistently wish for the same things; we constantly desire different goals, new items and then something else again. Often we didn't really mean to wish and were just intrigued for a moment, only to wish for something completely different the next minute. The cosmos doesn't mind. It delivers whatever is wished for, even though we might not need it at all any more. And suddenly we are dealing with a real mixture of sent wishes and lose control over our lives. All around us, countless different things are happening, often cancelling each other out, and, amidst this chaos, we are completely unaware that we actually created it all. On top of this are all of our unconscious wishes that we really don't want fulfilled.

Suddenly we are back where we didn't want to be any more. All sorts of things are happening, and we have no idea who ordered all this!

We do much better if we realize our first wishes in a very conscious way and give them direction and meaning by writing them down clearly.

2. Watch out for 'coincidences' and write them down

From now on we are simply more alert and write down everything we notice. A lot of it will not have much to do with our wish – but some things will.

If you always look in the direction from which you are expecting your delivery it's possible that you will miss it altogether. After all, you are only prepared for the ways and means of delivery that your limited imagination is able to picture. The Universe, however, is much more genial. We sometimes say that a miracle has happened because we are so surprised by the many 'coincidences' that have been happening in our lives in order to make our wish come true. In reality, all that has happened is that our wish has materialized. And it often happens in a way that we had not reckoned on.

3. Sharpen your intuition

Intuition often leads us to where we 'happen' to find the desired goal. Sometimes we overhear bits of a conversation containing some vital information for us. Sometimes we suddenly want to take a different way home from the usual one and 'happen' to encounter an old friend, who 'happens' to tell us about somebody we really should meet. And 'for some strange reason' this person has exactly what we want at that moment: a flat to let, the tools to unblock a drain, or a friend who is a wizard with computers.

If you wish to get in touch with your intuition, all you have to do is follow up what feels good and right for you. No matter how strange, embarrassing or ridiculous it might seem to us at first. Intuition is none other than acting spontaneously. If you get an idea of what you'd like to do – do it. Don't look for objections. Don't analyze it. Follow your impulse. With intuition you will act more spontaneously and your trust in your own perceptions will grow. Rather than tackling all the challenges in everyday life, allow yourself to drift towards the right solution. It is really nothing more than re-catching the minute particles of energy that we have sent out ourselves. And by returning to us, they will lead us to where we will receive the desired object or goal. Discover how wonderfully your intuition is guiding you by looking at the entries in your diary.

4. Recognize your doubts

In case your wishes don't come true, often there is a second wish which turns out to be stronger than the first one.

This second wish certainly counteracts the first one, is more persistent and has much more conviction behind it. Most of the time, this second wish is called doubt.

Quite often, a consciously expressed wish is superseded by an unconsciously doubtful thought. We can recognize how persistently this negative wish, a factual prevention, will influence our life by checking out how successful we are in our conscious wishing.

All the positive thinking, all mantras of the world won't help if deep inside us we constantly think of limitations and deprivation. Doubting is a deeply ingrained quality in some people, a firmly rooted belief which will come true, just as positive thinking will.

Working with 'doubt-ticks'

Every time we somehow feel some doubt regarding a wish, we put a little tick into our calendar. You will be amazed how many ticks will turn up there even after a short time. This only proves how strong our belief is that our wish will not be granted.

Doubts are not an entirely bad thing though, as long as you don't take them too seriously. If you refuse to focus much energy on them, their impact remains small.

It is best, therefore, to let the doubts come up and not to pay too much attention to them. There they are. They surface, are briefly looked at – after all they are only doubts which we won't pay much attention to – and are let go and sent on their way without any further comment.

Now you give every 'doubt-tick' another one that says

'No attention given'. You will be amazed how rapidly your doubts will disappear over a year. Instead, you will find a deeply rooted trust in your life.

Barbel's Method

Imagine that with every doubt-tick you would cancel out a doubt, and by ticking it you would rob it of all its power and energy! Then the many ticks in your calendar are little marks that indicate, like in the game of Battleships, that you have found and destroyed and sunk all those doubts. The more ticks, the more success-fully you have finally 'sunk' all your doubts.

5. Monitor your wishes

Have I got what I wished for???

Noting down your wishes and doubts in the calendar has another advantage. It is a fabulous way of proving success to yourself.

Because even after a short while we often don't know any more what exactly we have been wishing for. We vaguely remember the general drift, but more often than not the exact words have been jumbled up in our memory. That is not surprising as day after day countless new influences crowd our brain. Things change, our thoughts alter and so does our memory, which mirrors mostly an inseparable mixture of truths, thoughts and hopes.

When the order is delivered and you can read over exactly what you originally wished for, it will usually cause surprise.

You will be amazed at how your wish has been fulfilled exactly the way you initially wrote it down.

Now we can work on the original written-down wish. What did I get? Is it exactly what I wanted? If the answer is yes, hooray!! If not, which words do I need to alter? Why was it delivered differently? Which words were disadvantageous for the energy to be sent? We can phrase the wish better now and be more precise. What do we really want??

This method will enable us to master the art of wishing in no time at all.

On the next page are some hints and tips from Barbel's experience.

Cosmic Ordering

☆☆☆☆

Based on *The Cosmic Ordering Service* by Barbel Mohr

It is mostly unconscious thought patterns and doubts that hinder successful wishing. Just order it with the Universe! By using the verb 'to order', our unconscious associates a sense of naturally taking things for granted. It surely will be that way. When you write down your order in the diary, imagine that it is an email to the 'warehouse of the Universe'.

Then you do whatever you do after having placed any other order: you get back to what you were doing before and don't think about it any more.

You can reinforce this process by a little exercise in gratitude. This causes an automatic letting-go on the unconscious level. We focus our attention so that it is redirected towards 'gratefulness for little things' rather than leave it moping around and waiting for the wish's final arrival.

Imagine how it would be if you had the desired object already in your possession. How would you feel, what would your day look like, what would be different? Let yourself sink as deeply as possible into that feeling of how it would be. And as soon as you really feel it, say thank you for it. This is a powerful way of drawing all things desired into your life.

The Power of Togetherness

☆☆☆☆

The power of praying/wishing for others

In a well-known experiment at New York's Columbia University, 219 women with the so-far-unfulfilled desire to have a child underwent a double-blind experiment. While the overall conditions stayed the same, half of the women were prayed for, while the others were not; neither they nor their doctors were aware who was being prayed for. Half the women in the 'prayer group' became pregnant – twice as many as in the control group.

An article in *Avanti* in 2005 mentioned that, according to analysis by Dr Benson of Harvard, prayers work like a miracle cure and can actually raise life expectancy by as much as eleven years.

This is not so much about the content of the prayers. It's rather about the conviction that some higher or conscious universal power does exist and the intention to stay in actual close contact with it by praying, meditation or in any other way.

Together for everybody

By making use of these findings we can a) send our own wishes on our wishing dates to the cosmos, and b) make wishes for everybody as well as for the wellbeing of the planet as a whole.

My wish is that as many of you as possible will always finish your own particular orders with the words:

'… and I also wish that the wishes of all the people who are sending orders and wishes right now will be fulfilled too, for the ultimate wellbeing of everybody! I am sending my thanks, my love and my wishes for wellbeing to every area of the planet earth, nature and the whole of the Universe!'

Einstein shared this belief that nature has the tendency towards harmony. If all the people in the world would reconnect with their innermost nature and would thus find their own personal harmony and fulfilment, and if they would wish the same for everybody else, we would finally achieve worldwide peace! I am deeply convinced that this is true.

Your Monthly Date
with Yourself

☆☆☆☆

For every month, this calendar offers a wealth of information and topics. Now all you need is the time to actually deal with it.

That is simple enough! Make a date with yourself. Every month, put in an appointment with yourself. Whether this will be for two, three or five hours or for a whole day depends on how it will fit in with the rest of your life. With a bit of organization, two hours per month will be manageable even if you have five children.

Maybe you would like to start the date with yourself with a little exercise in self-love in front of the mirror. Then you can take the opportunity to reflect on the topics for the month and note down where you actually are at the moment and what direction to take next. Reflect in all honesty on the here and now, and love yourself in spite of it – or because of it.

Imagine your desired goal as vividly as possible, as if you had achieved it already. How would it feel? How would you be feeling? Write this down in your calendar and watch how things will develop.

You end your date with yourself by giving yourself a little treat. I'm not so much thinking of going shopping or watching TV, but rather of playing your favourite music or having a long soak.

Wishing Dates

There are certain dates in your calendar which are particularly auspicious for sending off wishes and for ordering!

These are astrologically determined wishing dates, turbo wishing dates chosen by a medium, and favourable wishing days according to the Mayan calendar.

Astrologically chosen wishing days

Some astrologically determined wishing days are the days of the New Moon. Wishing is possible all day long, but it works most powerfully half an hour after the New Moon and for the next two hours.

The Germans have a saying: 'When you count your money at New Moon, you'll never lack any.' And according to one of the Brothers Grimm, Estonians have a saying at the New Moon: 'I am greeting you, Moon, for you to grow old and for me to stay young.'

The New Moon empowers all wishes related to new beginnings and growth, for more money, better health, something new …

The Full Moon is the ideal time to let go of something, e.g. to say goodbye to a bad habit.

At other times there are astrologically favourable aspects regarding certain topics. Mostly these happen for several days in a row, and you can recognize them in the list of wishing days by the symbols representing certain aspects.

Turbo Wishing Days

Turbo dates have been chosen by a medium and are particularly powerful. Andreas Petersen 'sees' the whirls and eddies of energy in terms of time, and, according to him, there are special times in which nearly all life forces are briefly in balance. In his view, those times amplify the wishing power thousandfold because they reach the Universe with more power and energy. Accordingly, they can initiate more power and energy in return.

If you'd like to have your own personal ideal dates for wishing calculated, you can ring Andreas on +49 6151 999873. You'll find more information on Andreas at www.barbelmohr.de, under 'Heiler & Co.', a link on the home page. We don't charge for it, and Andreas does his energy treatment sessions, and lots more, for donations only. As they only last a few minutes, everybody participating makes his or her wish at the same time. This amplifies the power exactly as in a shared meditation. There is an exact time given with these dates, which should be stuck to.

Turbo Wishing Dates with Barbel and Pierre

Three times a year the symbol for a turbo wishing day bears two little extra stars. It means that at those times we, Barbel and Pierre, will also order and make wishes. For ourselves and everybody else.

Wishing dates in the Mayan calendar

The calendar of the Mayans is very old and has remained unaltered over thousands of years. It is different from our own Gregorian calendar, which was last changed in the sixteenth century. According to the Mayan calendar, the year begins on 26th July, not 1st January. The reason for this is that each and every year on this day there is a certain stellar constellation. On that day, our sun is in conjunction with our nearest central sun, Alcyone (in the Pleiad system) and the star Sirius B. The last day of the Mayan year is 24th July, and the remaining day, 25th July, is the so-called 'green day', a day outside time. It connects the dwindling year with the new one.

Johann Koessner (www.maya.at) is a renowned expert on the Mayan calendar. He claims that every person has his or her own 'green day', which is the day before one's birthday. It is a kind of personal day outside time, and is particularly well-suited for making wishes and initiating changes.

☆ ☆ ☆ ☆

One Affirmation a Day

☆☆☆☆

For each day in the calendar you will find a short sentence. These affirmations reflect the quality of the respective day. Using them, we can challenge unpleasantness or reinforce positive things in a very focused way.

Affirmations can help us to plan the day, and they remind us of our true nature. As long as we remind ourselves consciously of them during the day, we will stay focused and will be able to listen to our inner voice. Then everything is easier, and we can go with the flow.

Be playful with your affirmations, take them as a motto for the day and at the end of the day check what has changed as a result of this. You will find even after a short span of time that you live so much more consciously. This again has a positive impact on your wishing work, as you become more able to notice the little signs, the 'coincidences', which may be helping to make your wish come true.

Monthly Message

☆☆☆☆

Before the beginning of each month you will find in turn either a meditation by Pierre or a success story from one of Barbel's readers.

If you experience particularly wonderful things on the communal wishing dates in this calendar, please mail

Successful orders
These are meant to be inspirational, so that you think of numerous wonderful ideas rather than always simply ordering a suitable parking space! As the saying goes, 'No pain, no gain,' and that doesn't just apply to your muscle tone but also to your direct line to the Universe. 'The only difference between a genius and the average person is that the genius has discovered an inner light and Mr Average has not.' (From Walter Russell, the universal genius.) In this sense our success stories are meant to inspire you to communicate more often with your inner light.

HOT TIP Don't just appeal to the Universe in the event of problems, please also share your good times, such as in: 'Hey, Universe, did you see that? What wonderful fireworks! A laughing child! A fantastic success – it's soooo lovely, and I'm sending up some of my joy!' That, too, keeps those Universe communication lines running smoothly.

them to kalender@baerbelmohr.de, or to kalender@pierre-franckh.de. With a bit of luck your story will be printed somewhere, at some point, maybe even in next year's diary. With even more luck you will win one of three Christmas surprise parcels. In case you don't like surprises and would rather win a workshop on *joie de vivre* for two (the workshop is free), or a personal coaching session with Pierre, please let us know. Don't forget to give us your address …

In the event that your doubts gain the upper hand again after a time, just go back to the words. It will quickly guide you towards the desired energy.

Wishing Meditations

My book on successful wishing has been one of the most unexpected bestsellers of the last few years. It has changed the lives of many people in a very positive way. On my lecture tours and by email, people keep asking me whether there are any specific guidelines for wishing – some blueprint for the ultimately successful wish. Here is my answer:

Each and every wish is individual, and in personal coaching I look for specific words that will help the seeker to overcome his or her doubts. But there is a general and widely successful 'blueprint'. The following wishing meditations will guide you to a precisely defined stream of energy so that everything within you can be open to everything you would like to invite into your life.

It is recommended that at the end of each meditation on a wish you imagine in a very visual way your own personal desire. Whatever it may be, present it to your inner eye like a video clip and stay with the energy that was created by the meditation.

Key to Symbols

☆☆☆☆

 Turbo Wishing Date

 Turbo Wishing Date with Barbel and Pierre

 Health

 Wealth

 Job success (finding the right profession or position)

 Love relationships (finding a new partner or harmony with an existing one)

Sensual encounter

 Holidays

 Forgiveness (of others and oneself)

 Wellbeing and comfort at home (a new house/ flat, a new fridge, new wallpaper etc.)

 Children (harmony with children, solving school problems etc.)

 Letting go of old patterns

Weekly Diary
2007

☆☆☆☆

New Years Eve Wishes

☆☆☆☆

I look back to the year gone by with gratitude and joy.
I am thankful for all the wonderful events that I was
allowed to experience this last year. My thanks for each
and every day on which I was healthy and content; for
each and every day on which I had enough to eat and
to drink.

I am thankful for the days and the nights with my
friends and relatives. For their presence and willing-
ness to share their time with me.

I am grateful for all the trials and tribulations that
enabled me to grow and mature, in which I could
prove my strength and my abilities.

I am grateful for the love and tenderness I received
from so many different people.

I am thankful for the smile on my face, the alertness of
my mind and the love I could feel for others.

And now, with the wealth of those thoughts and the
depth of my gratitude, I focus on the year to come.

I am conscious that everything will turn out in my
best interest because I know that I will be cared for. I

am aware that my positive thoughts will make this world more beautiful and bountiful, and so I already feel the happiness that will be filling my life.

My happiness will begin at this very moment. Right now I am in the process of creating this wonderful world. I will cause changes in this world, I will enrich it and I will continue to focus my energy on all the beloved things and people in my surroundings.

I am full of beauty and inner riches, and I know that all this will manifest itself externally.

I am cared for, because I care for myself. Other people are close to me, because I am close to myself. This New Year is another step on the way to becoming more mature, more alert and conscious. Step by step I will approach my true nature.

All my wonderful thoughts will take shape now.

Begin to think of all the things that you desire. Imagine that everything you wish for has already entered your life: An enriching partnership. Inner wealth and material wealth. Health. Joy. Friends. Lightness of being. Laughter. A fulfilling job.

January 2007 week 1

1 monday

I'll plan my year in a generous and realistic way

2 tuesday

I recognize my emotional bonds and ties

3 wednesday

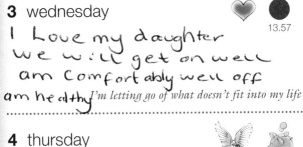

I Love my daughter
We will get on well
I am Comfortably well off
I am healthy

13.57

I'm letting go of what doesn't fit into my life

4 thursday

Deep feelings and ease can go together

friday **5**

My feelings lead me to my own truth

saturday **6**

I have the strength to offer protection and shelter to others

sunday **7**

If I trust the strength of my soul I will find healing

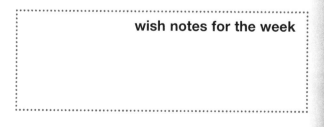

wish notes for the week

January 2007 week 2

8 monday

I can organize my life

9 tuesday

I am in control of my feelings

10 wednesday

I recognize that some things are allowed to be easy

11 thursday

The clearer I am, the more truthful my relationships will be

friday **12**

I voice my feelings

 saturday **13**

I explore everything in depth

sunday **14**

I integrate work and fun into my life

wish notes for the week

January 2007 week 3

....

15 monday

I can express myself clearly

....

16 tuesday

I give my life a well-defined structure

....

17 wednesday

I have the strength to manage my tasks

....

18 thursday

Today I am allowed to be a child

18.15-18.19   04.01

friday **19**

I give my wishes a clear structure

saturday **20**

I'll give myself a day that will be as easy as pie

sunday **21**

I have stamina under pressure

wish notes for the week

January 2007 week 4

22 monday

Everything new enriches my life

23 tuesday

I remain steadfast

24 wednesday

I am open to new feelings

25 thursday

I forgive myself and others

friday **26**

At home I feel safe and protected

saturday **27**

I am at one with nature

sunday **28**

My feelings and my actions are in harmony

wish notes for the week

January/February 2007 week 5

29 monday

I feel open to new ideas

30 tuesday

Calmness is power

31 wednesday

Today I will listen to my heart

1 thursday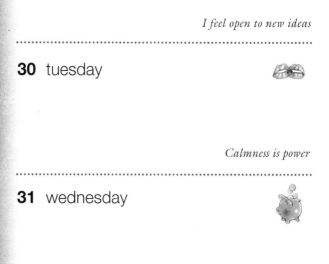

I follow my own ideas

05.45

friday **2**

I recognize my own worth

saturday **3**

I evaluate my situation realistically

sunday **4**

I have the stamina to deal with day-to-day life

wish notes for the week

Tickets for Wimbledon
— a Special Booking

☆☆☆☆

David, a dear friend of Manfred and me, loves tennis. For years he had been saying, 'Once, just once, I'd love to sit in Centre Court for the men's final!' Last year he entered his name into the public ballot for tickets – in good time. But the confirmation would not come. It seemed that again David would miss out on his dream. It looked like a good case for a cosmic order.

When David attended one of my workshops on 'Zest for Life', he made use of the heightened energy of a group order and sent a wish for a couple of tickets for the Wimbledon men's final into the Universe. His friends thought him crazy, because all the available tickets had been distributed for a while. But the Universe is very creative. David works as a consultant and coach for businessmen, and one of his usual clients asked him to coach the security guards for Wimbledon and other major events in dealing with conflicts amongst fans. Short refresher courses for the security people also take place directly before a big event, and so it happened that David not only saw the men's final, but the women's as well!

February 2007 week 6

5 monday

I concentrate on the necessary things

6 tuesday

My family gives me strength

7 wednesday

I trust in my guidance from above

8 thursday

I allow myself to express myself creatively

friday **9**

I am alive and like a child

saturday **10**

Every coincidence has a deeper meaning

sunday **11**

In silence I find myself

wish notes for the week

February 2007 week 7

12 monday

I trust in my powers

13 tuesday

I free myself from old ties

14 wednesday

I am as I am

15 thursday

My intuition shows me the way forward

week 7 2007 February

friday **16**

I am responsible for myself

16.14

saturday **17**

I use my energy to make successful wishes

sunday **18**

I respect other people's feelings

:::

wish notes for the week

:::

February 2007 week 8

19 monday

I discover my beauty

20 tuesday

I allow my creativity to flourish

21 wednesday

I live on my own inner strength

22 thursday

I am beautiful

05.23-05.24

friday **23**

I feel at ease with myself

saturday **24**

I am ready for new things

sunday **25**

I follow my inspiration

wish notes for the week

February/March 2007 week 9

26 monday

I give my inner child some space

27 tuesday

I recognize the power of freedom

28 wednesday

I accept the darker side in me

1 thursday

I enjoy life

23.17

friday **2**

I follow my intuition

saturday **3**

I give my creativity pride of place

sunday **4**

I stay with myself

wish notes for the week

Birthday Meditation

☆☆☆☆

*This day today is mostly for myself and for
my parents.*

*With deepest joy I thank my parents for bringing
me into this world and raising me.
They have done and given their best, just as I do
and give my best day after day.
Only because of their strength and sacrifices am
I able to be alive today.*

*The clearer I can see the love they have given to me,
The better I can be open to love myself.*

*Today is a good day
To recapture all the parts in me that I have forgotten
or repressed a long time ago.
All the inner children
I have left behind in disappointment and hurt
Are waiting, full of longing
That I take care of them again and integrate them
into my days.
They are part of me. My childlike joy,
My laughter, my zest
And my love.*

*All those parts that have always been mine
I will recapture because I forgive my parents
Everything that they have done to me.*

By forgiving them, I open up to the love in myself,
Which I had cut myself off from before.
By forgiving I give my inner children
Renewed attention and love.
I take them back,
I accept their love,
I am no longer cut off from life.
I am no longer cut off from myself.

Life opens up ahead of me in all its richness
It has always been there,
Only I did not feel part of it.

Through the love towards my parents,
I am again part of the circle of life
Life is waiting for me, because I have opened up.
It had always been there at my disposal,
Only today I am fully conscious of it.

I am thanking God, the Universe and the power
of my positive thoughts for the creation of a
wonderful New Year in which everything,
all that I ever wish for, is at my disposal.

Most of all and with all my heart I thank my parents.
Because of them,
I can be here today.

I love life, and life loves me.

March 2007 week 10

5 monday

Everything will be all right

6 tuesday

A Good Wishing Day.
A wonderful day to experience one's own beauty –
I am beautiful

7 wednesday

Spiritual insights give me strength

8 thursday

I meet everything with curiosity and openness

friday **9**

I recognize my true dreams

saturday **10**

I see beauty in every moment

sunday **11**

Everything is good and complete

wish notes for the week

March 2007 week 11

12 monday

I will challenge my fears

13 tuesday

I concentrate on my tasks

14 wednesday

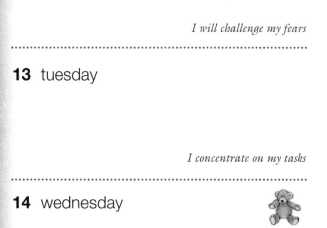

I trust in the rhythms of life

15 thursday

I introduce my visions into my reality

friday **16**

I trust my intuitions

saturday **17**

I express my feelings

◯
02.43

sunday **18**

I discover a pattern in my life

wish notes for the week

March 2007 week 12

....

19 monday

My male and my female sides are at ease with each other

....

20 tuesday

My inner balance is reflected on the outside

....

21 wednesday

I completely accept the female and male aspects of myself

....

22 thursday

I find my own truth deep inside myself

friday **23**

I see everything with fresh eyes

 saturday **24**

I am at ease with my intuition

 sunday **25**

I am aware of my masks

wish notes for the week

March 2007 week 13

26 monday

I allow myself to be inspired by new ideas

27 tuesday

I am true to myself

28 wednesday

I am acting on an inner sense

29 thursday

Clear structures help me to manage my life

friday **30**

I can let go of all old things

saturday **31**

I pursue my goals with determination

sunday **1**

I recognize how important my family is to me

wish notes for the week

Mimir Orders a Friend

☆☆☆☆

Susan, who is mad about animals, felt like taking up horse riding again. But she didn't want just any old horse, because she had developed a passion for Icelandic ponies. She also had a clear vision of how the stable was going to be: with a large paddock, because horses like space. A short wish was sent off, more unconsciously than not.

A short time later she asked at a livery that she 'happened' to pass by whether there were Icelandic ponies available. The answer of the stable's owner was: 'You're a god-send!' She had just received the request from the owner of the only Icelandic pony (out of 60 horses) in the stables to have the animal put down. It was a difficult horse that didn't like to be handled and had put several women off riding altogether.

Susan had a look at him and was captivated straight away. During the next few weeks, and with a lot of empathy and patience, she gained the animal's trust. There were a few difficulties. Today, however, she teaches children on Mimir, she goes on hacks with him all by herself – without any problems but with a lot of pleasure.

'I'd like to do more,' she said. 'Maybe I will put in a new order! I bought Mimir a year ago, and we have become real friends. He comes to me when I call him, and I have really grown to love him.'

The question is – who wished for whom???

April 2007 week 14

2 monday

17.15

I don't have to do everything by myself

3 tuesday

I know intuitively what to do

4 wednesday

I approach people in a proactive way

5 thursday

A Good Wishing Day.
A good day to realize major plans

week 14 2007 April

friday **6**

I set myself goals

saturday **7**

Today I'll motivate myself

sunday **8**

Everything works smoothly and fluently

wish notes for the week

April 2007 week 15

9 monday

Everything in good time

10 tuesday

I allow myself to be great

11 wednesday

I recognize my inner beauty

12 thursday

I allow myself my freedom

friday **13**

I support my friends

saturday **14**

I choose my own way

sunday **15**

What would you still want to do if this day were your last?

wish notes for the week

April 2007 week 16

16 monday

I consider other people's feelings

17 tuesday

11.36

I long for deep insights

18 wednesday

Tensions can also bring about positive changes

19 thursday

15.36-15.39

I tackle things

friday **20**

Challenges make me more mature

saturday **21**

My own clarity makes me grow

sunday **22**

I show my true self

wish notes for the week

April 2007 week 17

23 monday

I can look after myself

24 tuesday

I find new strength in a peaceful environment

25 wednesday

I love myself

26 thursday

Words can heal

friday **27**

I find myself in nature

saturday **28**

I have both my feet firmly on the ground

sunday **29**

I aim for harmony

wish notes for the week

April/May 2007 week 18

---

30 monday

I say yes to a harmonious relationship

---

1 tuesday

My body is a gift from God

---

2 wednesday

10.09

I am allowed to enjoy life

---

3 thursday

Today I will be very good to myself

friday **4**

There are creativity and beauty in everyday life too

saturday **5**

I will do something that I have never done before

sunday **6**

I love being on this planet

wish notes for the week

The Wish for a Wonderful Partner

☆☆☆☆

*I am now open and ready to let a deep
and fulfilling love into my life.
I create space and time in my life so my
wonderful partner will feel welcome.*

*At this very moment, my partner is just as willing
as me to enter into a wonderful relationship.*

*With the power of my thoughts I am drawing
a soulmate towards me. Our ways will cross with
the same inevitability as night follows day.*

*I will stop searching because I am deeply certain
that the energies of my cosmic order will manifest
themselves at this very moment.
Everything is prepared and ready in a most
wonderful way.*

*I know that the right partner for me exists
and will enter into my life.
I know that my partner is not perfect,
but he is perfect for me.
He will help me to recognize my own limitations,
to explore my faults and to work on them.
Through him I will get closer to myself, day after day,
week after week, year after year.
Through him I will get closer to myself
than would have been possible without him.*

*Through him I get in touch with my wonderful
deep self as well as with my unloved parts.
Because I am loving I am ready to show myself
in the way I really am.
My partner, too, is allowed to be himself.*

*Love is the driving and supporting power
in this relationship.
Because of my partner I grow and mature
and become great and am able to show this.*

*I show all my patience, my determination,
my loyalty, my fears and my fearlessness.*

I am ready to allow and tolerate closeness.

*I am open and free enough to accept the power of love.
I let go of everything that might restrict this
inner freedom. I let go of my idea of myself
as a single person and already consider myself
a partner in a fulfilling relationship.
My partner is in my life already.
He is there. I sense his presence.*

You are wholeheartedly welcome in my life.

May 2007 week 19

7 monday

Joy is my normal state of being

8 tuesday

I express my wishes

9 wednesday

I support myself with love

10 thursday

All power is within me

friday **11**

I dedicate a whole day to myself because I'm worth it

saturday **12**

I enjoy being on my own

sunday **13**

I enjoy my possessions

wish notes for the week

May 2007 week 20

14 monday

I enjoy the lightness in my life

15 tuesday

Every dream contains an unfulfilled desire

16 wednesday

19.27

Dreams can come true

17 thursday

I find truth only in myself

friday **18**

Friends enrich my life

saturday **19**

I positively enjoy my conscious mind

sunday **20**

I live life spontaneously, flexibly and freely

wish notes for the week

May 2007 week 21

21 monday

I am open and ready for a meaningful love relationship

22 tuesday

I create my own life

23 wednesday

I give myself a present

24 thursday

I love all parts of my personality

friday **2**5

I am pleased with my achievements

saturday **26**

Every challenge makes me stronger

sunday **27**

I pay attention to my body and give it enough exercise

wish notes for the week

May 2007 week 22

28 monday

Love finds its way through my heart

29 tuesday

I am alive and full of energy

30 wednesday

I am open and ready for changes

31 thursday

I can enjoy new things

01.04

friday **1**

I have the strength and the confidence to deal well with criticism

saturday **2**

There is a solution waiting for every problem

sunday **3**

I stand up for my ideals

wish notes for the week

An Ideal Partner

☆☆☆☆

For more than two years, Jessica has been very successful with her wishes. But even though she had been single for more than a year she had not dared to even approach this topic. With a wry smile she confesses: 'I am not that easy. I am 25, had a Harley-Davidson for three years (that was a cosmic order, too!) and have an old-fashioned attitude towards relationships – but maybe it's quite normal? I need a partner who will come with me on my motorbike and also to the biker conventions. But I also want him to be able to feel at ease in a posh hotel.' Well, no Mr Right was in sight. So she tried a cosmic order. 'I would like a man who at this point in time is absolutely suited to me. You up there will know exactly what I need.' The delivery came immediately. Now she only has one 'problem': 'Them up there are really clever, and they really listen. I have always said that I would stop smoking if my boyfriend was a non-smoker. And what have I got now? A biker who doesn't smoke! Which is unusual, because at the biker conventions 99% of all the people smoke. When I'm with him I lose all interest in cigarettes, but in other surroundings it is quite difficult. I guess I need more help from above to really quit.'

June 2007 week 23

4 monday

Even the smallest element is rich in itself

5 tuesday

I am open to new influences

6 wednesday

New things develop out of the blue

7 thursday

03.16-03.19

I am open to emotionally deep conversations

friday **8**

I discover my inner strength

saturday **9**

I trust in my inner guidance

sunday **10**

I express my feelings openly and honestly

wish notes for the week

June 2007 week 24

11 monday

I focus on my creativity

12 tuesday

Limitations are only in my mind

13 wednesday

There are adventures to discover in everyday life

14 thursday

I am joyful and relaxed

friday **15**

03.13

I tempt myself to follow new directions

 saturday **16**

Today I learned something new

sunday **17**

I am part of a whole and interact with it powerfully

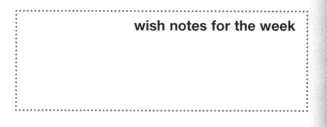

wish notes for the week

June 2007 week 25

18 monday

I enjoy being creative

19 tuesday

I am open to creative intuition

20 wednesday

I discover the power of words

21 thursday

I love my life with all my heart

friday **22**

New friends bring new inspiration

saturday **23**

I enchant my surroundings

sunday **24**

I am curious for happiness

wish notes for the week

June 2007 week 26

25 monday

I listen to my gut feelings

26 tuesday

I am continuously looking for new things

27 wednesday

This day is waiting especially for me

28 thursday

I allow my feelings to inspire me

friday **29**

I follow a new dream

saturday **30**

13.49

I enjoy my energy

sunday **1**

I can trust my feelings

wish notes for the week

Wishing for Wealth

☆ ☆ ☆ ☆

I am open and ready to let money into my life.
I create some space, a window in my life so that the
wonderful power of riches will feel welcomed by me.

First and foremost I am deeply convinced
that I am entitled to have money.
From now on I have a different view of wealth.
Money is a fantastic element in my life.
Money is a sign of my inner richness.
Money is an expression of my zest for life
and shows the flow of my life energy, which I am
directing now towards this goal.
Money is just as natural in my life as food,
drink and sleep.

Through the power of my thoughts I am drawing
now the comforting feeling of wealth into my life.
I am thoroughly convinced that the energies of the
wish I am sending out will manifest themselves
at this very moment.
Everything exists in abundance.
For everybody. And so for me too.
I am inviting it into my life.

I am open and free in dealing with money. I let go of
everything that could curtail this inner freedom.

*I let go of my concept of shortage and consider myself,
at this very moment, as blissfully rich.
In a wondrous way, money already has a place
in my life. It surrounds me in an enriching way.*

*Wealth is unconditionally welcome in my life.
I thank God, the Universe and the power of my
positive thoughts for the granting of this wish.*

Option:

*Consider what exactly you want money for
and express this as a precise order.*

*The Universe is boundlessly creative. It knows
so many more ways to achieve what is desired than
buying it with money.
While you are waiting for the delivery, practise
gratefully accepting everything that comes to you
– money and gifts and presents of all kinds.
And practise parting with everything, be it
money or objects, with joy and gratefulness.
Thus you create abundance.
If you have negative feelings when receiving or
giving money and other things, you might think
unconsciously that it would be better to have less
because you wouldn't be feeling bad so often.
For this reason, give and take everything with joy!*

July 2007 week 27

2 monday

Traditions can also make you feel safe

3 tuesday

I am at home with myself

4 wednesday

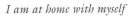

Friends enrich my life

5 thursday

I declare myself

friday **6**

I am ready for closeness

saturday **7**

I trust in my creativity

sunday **8**

My feelings lead me to the right place

wish notes for the week

July 2007 week 28

9 monday

I am amazed by miracles every day

10 tuesday

I am receptive and expressive

11 wednesday

I share my feelings

12 thursday

My enthusiasm is convincing

friday **13**

I have a sense for good opportunities

 ○
12.04

saturday **14**

I dedicate today to fantasy and imagination

sunday **15**

I write down my dreams

wish notes for the week

July 2007 week 29

16 monday

I am conscious of my inner strength

17 tuesday

I make use of my intuition at work, too

18 wednesday

I believe in my beliefs

19 thursday

I draw strength from my roots

friday **20**

I experience my feelings consciously

saturday **21**

I thank my parents for everything

sunday **22**

My life is valuable

wish notes for the week

July 2007 week 30

23 monday

I am allowed to be insecure at times

24 tuesday

Today I look after my inner child

25 wednesday

4.15-4.19
14.15-14.19

I am flooded by waves of love

26 thursday

My feelings contain the whole truth

friday **27**

I have an inner sense of the best decision

13.48-13.50

saturday **28**

I put myself first

sunday **29**

I experience my inner world through my dreams

wish notes for the week

July/August 2007 week 31

30 monday

00.48

I am all feelings today

31 tuesday

Today I focus on my body

1 wednesday

My own style gives me strength

2 thursday

I am proud of what I have achieved

friday **3**

I am able to achieve my goals

saturday **4**

I feel like a queen or king

sunday **5**

I create my own world

wish notes for the week

Dream House Wanted

☆☆☆☆

For over a year Mandy had been looking for a flat, but all the properties she had viewed had left her undecided. One Saturday morning, when still in bed, she pondered at length about what the reason could be that she still had not found the right place.

All year long she had been convinced that she only could afford the cheapest flat in a rundown block and had concentrated her search on just that. But she didn't really want to live like that.

But what did she want? Mandy started a list of her dream house: It should be in a nice, leafy area but fairly close to her place of work. It should have a fitted kitchen. She wanted it big and light, with wooden floors and an extra room for practising the piano, because she is a piano teacher. Mandy smiled a bitter-sweet smile while thinking of the millionaire husband of her dreams who seemed to refuse to enter into her life. Then she tried an order.

The next morning, a Sunday, she drove to school to prepare a project for the coming week. Shortly before she got there she remembered the order she had placed the day before. Without another thought she turned off into a narrow side street she had never taken before. Three seconds later she stopped at a garden gate with a large cardboard sign: 'Flat to let with garden and studio.' The rest of the description can be found in the wish list above. The landlord happened to be in the garden. Mandy approached him, they sat down in his living room, and three minutes later they agreed on a contract. All possible without a millionaire husband.

August 2007 week 32

6 monday

I contemplate the world in its infinite variety

7 tuesday

I discover my authority

8 wednesday

I have endless capabilities

9 thursday

I dedicate this day to my joy

friday **10**

Today I will speak only positively about others

saturday **11**

I am full of joie de vivre

   ◯
23.02

sunday **12**

I am proud of my success

> **wish notes for the week**

August 2007 week 33

13 monday

I can be careful with my energy

14 tuesday

I am pleased when I achieve something

15 wednesday

I am full of childlike impatience

16 thursday

Responsibilities are fun

friday **17**

I reach my targets

saturday **18**

Goals can be reached in a playful way

sunday **19**

Life for me is a cornucopia of abundance

wish notes for the week

August 2007 week 34

20 monday

I discover new aspects in myself all the time

21 tuesday

I dedicate today to my (inner) children

22 wednesday

My creativity always finds the best solution

23 thursday

I am a source of inspiration

friday **24**

I can express my inner self

saturday **25**

I give this day a clear direction

sunday **26**

I bring more colour into my life

wish notes for the week

August 2007 week 35

27 monday

I show my inner wealth

28 tuesday

10.35

I find the right voice because it is in me

29 wednesday

I am special

30 thursday

I can stand by myself

friday **31**

Treating others with care and consideration makes me feel good

saturday **1**

I am grateful for my life

sunday **2**

I accept myself as I am

wish notes for the week

The Wish for a Satisfying Job

☆☆☆☆

I am open and ready to let a truly satisfying job into my life now. Most of all I am deeply convinced that I am entitled to be in the right workplace.

From now on I look at my work with different eyes. My work is an expression of my zest for life and my creativity. Through my work I discover my hidden talents and can make use of them. I feel relaxed and enriched in my job and enrich others by the power of my actions. Others and I experience acknowledgement and happiness through my work. My work is wanted and appreciated.

I am free and strong enough to do justice to the right kind of job. I let go of everything that could restrict this inner freedom. I let go of the concept of shortcomings and see myself committed to a fulfilling job right now.

Through the power of my thoughts I am drawing my ideal business partners and colleagues towards me. I am deeply convinced that the energies of my wish are manifesting themselves at this very moment.

Everything is prepared in a wondrously perfect way.
There is already the ideal workplace for me.
My business partners, my colleagues and employers are
as prepared as I am at this very moment to commit
themselves to me as a great worker.
The right job is unconditionally welcomed in my life.

I thank God, the Universe and the power of my positive
thoughts for the fulfillment of my wish.

September 2007 week 36

3 monday

I learn from negative events

4 tuesday

I have achieved something in this life

5 wednesday

I am proud of myself

6 thursday

I can accept changes

friday **7**

Today I am thankful for my wealth

saturday **8**

I don't have to be perfect in everything

sunday **9**

I am allowed to rest at times

wish notes for the week

September 2007 week 37

10 monday

I am realistic

11 tuesday
12.44

Today I am thankful for my body

12 wednesday

I let go of old things

13 thursday

Meaningful conversations bring me joy

week 37 2007 September

friday **14**

Every mistake has a deeper meaning for me

saturday **15**

Today I am thankful for all relationships

sunday **16**

Today I feel loved by everybody

wish notes for the week

September 2007 week 38

17 monday

I follow my intuition

18 tuesday

I strive for mental clarity

19 wednesday

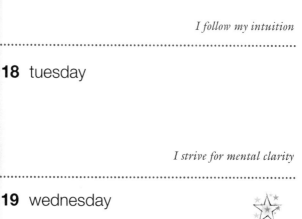

18.15-18.19

Today I give my life more structure

20 thursday

I am mindful in carrying out everyday chores

week 38 2007 September

friday **21**

I love my life

saturday **22**

Power rests in complete silence

sunday **23**

I realize my dreams

wish notes for the week

September 2007 week 39

24 monday

I give myself a present because I am worth it

25 tuesday

I pay attention to my inner child

26 wednesday

19.45

I face my fears with courage

27 thursday

I discover a different point of view

friday **28**

I thank my family

saturday **29**

I pay attention to achieving inner balance

sunday **30**

I can face the truth

wish notes for the week

Alex Gets Lost

☆☆☆☆

Alex, the owner of a small building company, was planning to have a site prepared for the erection of a new warehouse. He told his secretary to ask for some quotes, but when he saw the suggested price, he went pale. 'For that money I might as well buy a digger,' he thought and asked his secretary to find out about prices. But again, he could only shake his head about the sums involved. So he thought that this would be an opportunity to try out an order. 'Dear Universe, I am ordering a secondhand JCB for a few hundred quid.'

A short time later he visited a trade fair in a different part of the country. He finished what he had intended to do early and thought he might visit an old friend who lived nearby. He made a phone call, and found that the friend was at home. He asked whether Alex remembered the way to his house. Alex was sure he could find it and set off without asking for further instructions.

But, hey, someone must have muddled up his memory, because he suddenly found himself in a run-down area with only rough tracks instead of roads. That surely was not the right way to his friend's house. He turned around a corner – and what was sitting right in front of him by the side of the track? An old JCB.

Alex became excited. 'Maybe it's meant for me?' he asked himself and stopped. Someone emerged from an old shed nearby and walked towards his car. 'Do you want her?' the man asked. 'You can have her cheap.'

The price was right, and shortly afterwards Alex was the proud owner of a lovely digger. Now he could prepare the ground for the new warehouse himself. Since then years have gone by, but Alex has learned something from this successful order. 'Whenever I come across difficulties now, I remain calm and think to myself: there will be a solution. If the thing with the digger worked out, everything will work out. All you have to do is trust in it.'

October 2007 week 40

1 monday

My relationships are my best teachers

2 tuesday

I work for my own best interest

3 wednesday

I am open for new ideas

4 thursday

Resolving a conflict brings out true strengths

friday **5**

The best solution is one where everybody wins

saturday **6**

I am grateful for the beauty that surrounds me

sunday **7**

I am assertive with my goals

wish notes for the week

October 2007 week 41

8 monday

I explore things thoroughly

9 tuesday

I only watch out for the goodness in others

10 wednesday

I appreciate honest communication

11 thursday

○
05.01

I gain strength from harmony

friday **12**

I am generous and charming

saturday **13**

I approach everything with a smile

sunday **14**

My spiritual growth is important to me

wish notes for the week

October 2007 week 42

15 monday

I am grateful for the richness of my life

16 tuesday

I am aware of strength in my friends

17 wednesday

I create balance in my surroundings

18 thursday

My home is the expression of my inner contentment

friday **19**

I discover myself in my projections

saturday **20**

I dress according to the way I feel

sunday **21**

I appreciate everybody in their uniqueness

wish notes for the week

October 2007 week 43

22 monday

My sensuality is an expression of my zest for life

23 tuesday

04.05-04.10

I can solve every conflict

24 wednesday

I stand by my decisions

25 thursday

Today I surround myself with beauty

04.51

friday **26**

I am myself, even in conflict

saturday **27**

Today I am receptive to new influences

sunday **28**

I sense and discover my surroundings

wish notes for the week

October/November 2007 week 44

29 monday

I am in perfect harmony with myself and others

30 tuesday

I give this day to a friend

31 wednesday

The person opposite is my mirror image

1 thursday

I check whether I control other people

friday **2**

Every day is a day of transformation

saturday **3**

I pursue my goals with steadfastness

sunday **4**

Old beliefs only work so long as I cling to them

wish notes for the week

An Exercise in Beauty

☆☆☆☆

Take a quiet moment, turn the telephone off and choose a place in your home where you can remain undisturbed for quite a while. Some soft lighting would be good, and you need a large mirror. Maybe take the one from the hallway or the bathroom. Now sit down in front of the mirror. It's best to be naked. What would happen normally? We would immediately focus on our flaws. We are too fat, too flabby, too wrinkly, too old, too small, too pale, too unfit, too large. We invariably concentrate on our cellulite, the rolls of excess fat, the spots. We really are our own worst critics!

But today it will be different. Today we look at our image all calm and relaxed. No judging, please. We watch how we breathe, we contemplate our skin, the joints. We sense the warmth and the intimacy of the moment. This is our body which works so hard for us. Every minute, every day it is there for us. It never gives up. No matter how we maltreat it and force it. Regardless of how we insult and abuse it. Our body is wonderful. Without it we could not experience this wonderful life at all.

For a few minutes we give our body our wholehearted attention and appreciate its relentless work. We feel deep gratitude for our body.

After a few moments we focus our attention on the parts that we like in our body. Maybe it is your hair, your mouth, your shoulders, one particular finger, your left big toe, your breasts or your bottom. Maybe it is 'only' your navel. There will always be something that we like about our body. And now we concentrate on it while we confirm:

'I am open and ready to have my wish for beauty manifesting itself. Now I can let miracles into my life. I know that all my negative thoughts are not really mine and that they get weaker and weaker by the day. I love my body and look at it full of admiration. I am beautiful and desirable. And I am entitled to be like that.'

November 2007 week 45

5 monday

I am creative

6 tuesday

I act with feelings and energy

7 wednesday

I discover a new aspect of me

8 thursday

I confidently cross inner barriers

23.03

friday **9**

The more I let go, the more freedom I gain

saturday **10**

All day I do many things differently

sunday **11**

Who am I really?

wish notes for the week

November 2007 week 46

12 monday

Today I am convincing

13 tuesday

I let go of control

14 wednesday

I look for a new meaning

15 thursday

I look at my darker side with affection

week 46 2007 November

friday **16**

Forgiveness is the fastest way to one's own happiness

saturday **17**

I part with something to have room for something new

sunday **18**

I recognize parts of me that are still extreme

wish notes for the week

November 2007 week 47

19 monday

I create my own reality

20 tuesday

I shed an old skin

21 wednesday

People carry their burden until they drop it

22 thursday

Junk paralyses

friday **23**

I am open to new ideas

14.30

saturday **24**

Today I look at my inner struggles and let them go

sunday **25**

I make use of the power of my thoughts

wish notes for the week

November 2007 week 48

26 monday

I discover how I really am

27 tuesday

I accept my sensuous side

28 wednesday

I go my way alone

29 thursday

I take part proactively

friday **30**

I let go of a fear

 saturday **1**

Today I give myself more freedom

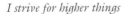 sunday **2**

I strive for higher things

wish notes for the week

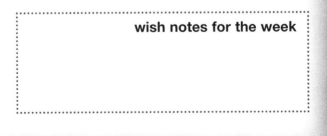

The Car Repair

☆☆☆☆

Rebecca had just moved house and was financially maxed out. On top of that, her car had broken down. Her order was: 'Dear Universe, I wish that somebody would be so kind as to pay for my car repair.'

A few days later the doorbell rang at quarter to seven in the morning. She had just taken a shower and done her ironing, but her hair still wet. She pretended not to have heard it, as she didn't want to answer the door looking like that. But the bell kept ringing. Finally someone actually knocked hard and said: 'Open the door, it's the police. We would like to ask you some questions.' The shocked Rebecca hectically looked for something to put on, ran to the door, flung it open and, hands raised above her head, called: 'It wasn't me!'

The two policemen just laughed.

But it wasn't her who had done something wrong. It turned out that someone had crashed into her car, which was parked in front of the house, had caused serious damage to the bodywork and had driven off. To her luck, a neighbour had watched the incident and remembered the number plate.

The insurance company of the perpetrator had the damage assessed and paid rather a lot of money for the repair. Rebecca had a choice of garages to have it done and went to the mechanic who usually looked after her car. The insurance money not only covered the body-work, but the engine repair as well. The Universe had indeed found somebody else to pay for her car repair.

December 2007 week 49

3 monday

I accept myself with love

4 tuesday

I utilize the strength of my belief

5 wednesday

I pursue my goals with optimism

6 thursday

I can clarify my ideals

15.18-15.22

friday **7**

I am delighted by my independence

saturday **8**

I gain strength from my knowledge

17.40

sunday **9**

I see something special in every person

wish notes for the week

December 2007 week 50

10 monday

I recognize my deepest desires

11 tuesday

Today I get to know the world anew

12 wednesday

I am honest with myself

13 thursday

Every day is the ideal day

friday **14**

I show my best side

saturday **15**

I recognize the goodness in people

sunday **16**

I benevolently look back on my life

wish notes for the week

December 2007 week 51

17 monday

I dedicate today to my inner wisdom

18 tuesday

I achieve all things I really want

19 wednesday

I create an ideal life for me

20 thursday

Today I really believe in myself

friday **21**

I give this day a special meaning

saturday **22**

I continuously make my life better

sunday **23**

I courageously step into new areas

wish notes for the week

December 2007 week 52

24 monday

01.16

I dedicate this day to my beliefs

25 tuesday

I live wholly from the heart

26 wednesday

I get in touch with my angel

27 thursday

I am loving and forgiving

week 52 2007 December

friday **28**

I dedicate this day to looking back on the year gone

saturday **29**

I am allowed to come first

sunday **30**

Every day enriches both me and others

wish notes for the week

31 monday

22.12-22.15

I look ahead courageously

1 tuesday

0.15-0.19

I search for beauty

2 wednesday

I handle stress creatively and playfully

3 thursday

I make sure to recognize connections

My List of Wishes

☆☆☆☆

_____

_____

_____

_____

_____

_____

_____

_____

_____

_____

_____

_____

_____

_____

And How They Came True

☆☆☆☆

My List of Wishes

☆☆☆☆

And How They Came True

☆☆☆☆

My List of Wishes

☆☆☆☆

And How They Came True

☆☆☆☆

List of Turbo Wishing Dates

☆☆☆☆

List of Turbo Wishing Dates

☆☆☆☆

We hope you enjoyed this Hay House book.
If you would like to receive a free catalogue featuring additional
Hay House books and products, or if you would like information
about the Hay Foundation, please contact:

Hay House UK Ltd
292B Kensal Rd • London W10 5BE
Tel: (44) 20 8962 1230; Fax: (44) 20 8962 1239
www.hayhouse.co.uk

***

Published and distributed in the United States of America by:
Hay House, Inc. • PO Box 5100 • Carlsbad, CA 92018-5100
Tel: (1) 760 431 7695 or (800) 654 5126;
Fax: (1) 760 431 6948 or (800) 650 5115
www.hayhouse.com

Published and distributed in Australia by:
Hay House Australia Ltd • 18/36 Ralph St • Alexandria NSW 2015
Tel: (61) 2 9669 4299 • Fax: (61) 2 9669 4144
www.hayhouse.com.au

Published and distributed in the Republic of South Africa by:
Hay House SA (Pty) Ltd • PO Box 990 • Witkoppen 2068
Tel/Fax: (27) 11 706 6612 • orders@psdprom.co.za

Distributed in Canada by:
Raincoast • 9050 Shaughnessy St • Vancouver, BC V6P 6E5
Tel: (1) 604 323 7100 • Fax: (1) 604 323 2600

***

Sign up via the Hay House UK website to receive the Hay House
online newsletter and stay informed about what's going on with
your favourite authors. You'll receive bimonthly announcements
about discounts and offers, special events, product highlights,
free excerpts, giveaways, and more!
www.hayhouse.co.uk